a collection of letters for the journey

along
the
way

Nikki Banas

Along the Way

for you, *my beautiful friend*,
may you find everything you are looking for
not just at the top of your mountain,
but all *along the way* too.

CONTENTS

INTRODUCTION

You will embark on countless unique, life-changing, and transformative journeys throughout your life. Some will last a lifetime and some may last just a season. Some of them will begin by complete surprise and others will be carefully planned out and measured from the beginning. Sometimes, you will not even realize that you are on a new path until you are well on your way. Some paths you will wish you could walk forever and some you will wish came to an end much sooner. Some will be full of wonderful highs and others will test your strength and courage through its lows. Whether the path you are on right now is easy or difficult, whether it is clear or foggy, whether you are trekking alone or with others, know that there is always, *always*, so much light, love, magic, and wonder to be found all along the way. So keep your eyes wide, your heart open, and allow yourself to experience all of the beautiful things this life has to offer along the way.

1. THE PATH AHEAD

your unique path

Your path through life is so incredibly unique to *you*. It will not look like any path that anyone has ever taken, nor like any path that anyone will ever take. Your path is yours alone, my beautiful friend. Your path is yours to walk, yours to create meaning and purpose. It is yours to walk with boundless joy and radiating love. And what makes your path so meaningful is that it is truly your own. No one else can walk it for you. Others can stand beside you, cheer for you, and be there to help you through, but at the end of the day, *you* are the one walking your path.

it's all yours

You are the one living and writing your story. You are the one experiencing all of your joys and pains. My beautiful friend, you are the one who earns your triumphs and victories. You are the one who has to give it everything you have to climb your mountains. And you are the one who has to face your losses and defeats too. You are the one who has to come face to face and be honest with yourself when you make a mistake. You are the one who has to learn how to heal and find inner peace after going through the dark. Others can encourage you and help you heal. They can help you grow and expand. They can help you navigate through your challenges and overcome your defeats. They can help you triumph and win your victories. But ultimately, *you* are the one guiding your life's direction. You are the one in charge of what you do with your one extraordinary life. My beautiful friend, you get to decide, and create, and walk, and *live* your incredibly unique path.

What you do with your
one extraordinary life
is entirely up to you, my beautiful friend.

shaping your path

The path you have taken has been shaped by your deep roots and where you come from. It has been shaped by the people you have met, the books you have read, the places you have explored, and the stories you have heard. Your path has been shaped by those who have inspired you and the teachers who have impacted you. It has been shaped by the ones you have loved and the ones who have loved you. It has been shaped by the things that make you come alive and the dreams buried in your heart. And the path ahead of you?

My sweet friend, that is the best part. The path ahead of you is entirely up to *you*. It has yet to be shaped. It is still untouched. Unformed. Wild... You get to decide the roads you take and the trails you explore. The mountains you climb and the oceans you sail. The cities you travel to and the cultures you explore. Who you bring alongside you and what you carry with you. Where you call home and how you spend your Sunday evenings. You get to shape it all. You can keep everything just as it is now, or you can decide to change it all and begin shaping a brand new path. Everything behind you is a little piece of you, but it does not dictate everything that lays ahead of you, my sweet friend. Everything ahead is entirely for you to shape.

forging a new path

Some paths that you take in life will already be forged by those who came before you, but some paths will need to be forged. My beautiful friend, never be afraid of going where there is no trail and leaving your own. Never be afraid to sail uncharted waters simply because no one else has sailed them before. Never be afraid to follow your heart off the beaten path to head in a brand new direction. If you ever come to a place where the path you are walking does not make you come alive, or it does not fill you with the excitement or adventure that you are looking for, do not be afraid to steer away and head off in a brand new direction. Do not be afraid to do something that has never been done before.

My beautiful friend, your path is not meant to look like anyone else's. It never has and it never will. Your path is shaped by you— and you are so uniquely and wonderfully *you*. Your path will not look like anyone else's because you are not doing what they are doing. They do not see the world in the exact same way as you do. You see it through your eyes and your lenses of the world. You have different dreams buried within you and different ideas of the life you want to live. And sometimes you will have to leave the well worn trail to forge your own way to find out where you truly belong. So forge your own path. Walk it how only you can. Run your path, my beautiful friend, dance freely as you go. Live your path how you want to live it. And know that as you create new ways and leave new trails, you are not just forging the path for yourself. You are blazing a trail for countless behind you too.

entirely yours

The path you choose to walk is for you, my beautiful friend. You do not need to explain why you are taking the direction that you are or justify each turn. You do not need to fit into any mold or into any box. My beautiful friend, there is no box. There is no ceiling. There is no limit to the life you can create— to the life that you can live. To the immense and deep joy that you can feel. To the wild dreams that you can bring to life. The path you walk is for no one else. It is for your beautiful soul and the things it aches for. You do not need approval or permission to live your life how you choose. You do not need to wait for anyone to let you know it is okay. And if you were waiting, my beautiful friend here it is: You are allowed to walk your path exactly how you want. You are allowed to chase your dreams no matter how far away they may seem. You are allowed to follow the sound of your own beating heart rather than the hum of the crowd. And others will not always understand. But that is okay. You are not walking this path for them. You are walking if for *you*.

Choose the path in life that make your soul come alive.

winding roads

Your path will not go in a perfectly planned-out straight line. It will twist and curve. It will force you to circle back and start over again and again. It will be incredibly tough in some moments, forcing you to summon all of your strength to make it through. And it will be breathtakingly beautiful in other moments, showing you just how incredibly beautiful this life is.

There really is no easy, straightforward, clear-cut path for navigating through all of the waves that life brings. There is no simple blueprint or map that outlines how it is all supposed to unfold or what to do when. Life throws unexpected and unpredictable storms at you. It gives you things that you were never expecting and does not give you the things that you have been praying for. It gives you the right people at the wrong time. It gives you the right opportunity but you miss it. It gives you battles that you could have never expected to have to fight. But it also brings moments that give you so much sunshine that they change who you are forever. It brings you horizons that you never could have dreamed of and skylines that leave you breathless.

So as you ride through the wild twists and the unexpected turns, remember that things do not have to go in a perfectly straight line to still have so much joy and love and purpose in them. Even among the wild twists and turns, the ups and downs, the hills and valleys, there is so much light to find. Look for those things, my sweet friend. Keep your eyes open to seeing all of the good around you. Keep your heart open to experiencing all of the light. Keep your soul set on feeling the warmth of the shining sun. Keep your head held high, especially during the moments when you are going through the lows and the valleys and the darkest nights. Keep your eyes up on the sun and all of the stars shining above you. Keep looking ahead knowing that there are beautiful mountaintops and views ahead. Because amidst it all, this life is a precious gift to each of us. Even during the downs, this life is still so boundlessly beautiful.

what you deserve

No matter what path you choose to walk through life, make sure it is the one that you want to travel. Not the path you think you should take or the one that will win other's approval, but the one that your heart and soul desire. The one that sparks a fire within your soul and lights up your entire world. You can walk a well worn path and make it beautifully your own. You can stray away from the one well worn and create your own new direction entirely. And you can change your path as often as your heart desires too. You can switch your direction over and over until you find the one you are meant to follow. You can take countless turns to experience everything around you. You can drift away and return over and over again. No matter the directions you take, always choose the ones that light a fire in you. Choose the ones that spark a fire inside your belly for the future you are creating. Walk the path that makes you feel the most alive. Because my sweet friend, that is the path through life that you deserve.

You deserve a life that you cannot wait to wake up to.

becoming you

As you shape the path that you take through life, your path will shape you too, my beautiful friend. When you visit new countries and new cities, you will see the place you call home a little bit differently. You will notice more about the things you never thought about before and wonder why you do things the way you do. And like the places you visit will shape you, the people you surround yourself with will shape you too. The songs you listen to and the books you read will impact you. The things you consume online and on T.V. will make a little difference on you too.

My beautiful friend, the path you take will help you become even more you. The teachers and coaches and people you admire will inspire you to keep growing and shining the glow that only you have. Your path will help you learn what really matters to you and who you care about. You will find out what you are willing to risk for your happiness. Your path will give you tough decisions to make. The storms you face will force you out of your comfort zone to become stronger.

They will make you question things you never thought to question. They will cause you to rethink things that you thought were solid. And the good times will change you too. The days full of sunshine. The seasons of endless blooms. They will show you what you are meant for. What you truly deserve in life... The boundless joy. The deep laugher and unconditional love. The lightness and freedom of life. It will all change you. So walk with your heart wide open for everything out there for you to experience.

surrender

My beautiful friend, surrender to the path that is meant for you. Surrender to this path that you are traveling, even if you thought it would be different. Even if you expected it to be so wildly different by now. Even if it is not the life you thought you would be living right now. Even if it is so far from it. Surrender to everything that is right in front of you, everything that is right and wonderful— *and* everything that is imperfect and messy and confusing. And know that surrendering does not mean you are giving up. Not at all. My beautiful friend, it means you are giving *in* to everything that is you. The good and the bad. The clean and the messy. It is giving in to the life right in front of you so that it can become the life you dream of. It is giving in to your true self and your true being. It is being honest with your heart and soul. It is trusting your intuition and gut feelings even when you cannot fully understand them. It is accepting the path that led you here no matter how difficult and gut-wrenching it was and accepting that you are here now. Because when you do surrender to your true self, your path ahead becomes clearer. The things not meant for you can fall away because you know that they are simply not yours. And in turn, your world opens up to everything that is meant for you. You become aligned to your true center. You find peace in knowing that you are on your own path, and that there is nowhere else you are supposed to be.

The universe has its own
timeline for you,
and it does not always
match your own.

Nikki Banas

uncovering

Your path will uncover itself in its own time— not always when you would like it to— *but it will.* The answers you are looking for will eventually make their way around to you. The things that do not make sense will eventually make sense. You will see that the heartbreaks, the failures, and the defeats were steering you in a new direction towards something so much better. You will see why things did not work out like you had planned. Your path *will* uncover itself, my beautiful friend. And until it does, keep looking for all of the good and light right around you— there is so much there for you. Keep looking for joy in the moments of not understanding. Keep looking for reasons to smile in the moments of doubt. You do not need to have all the answers or know how it will all unfold later to still find boundless grace and thankfulness for this moment.

bravely forward

My sweet friend, this path is yours. So as you make your way along your winding roads, give yourself grace for doing the best that you can with what you have. Give yourself plenty of space to learn and discover and grow and stretch. Give yourself kindness even when you tumble or make mistakes— you are simply human. Give yourself time to enjoy all of the beautiful twists and turns, and all of the breathtaking views along the way. Give yourself love for all of the winding roads that you have already traversed and love for all of the winding roads that you are about to travel. Keep your head held high through every up and every down. Walk your beautifully unique path in the way that only you can. My sweet friend, go bravely forward towards the life that is waiting for you.

2. THINGS TO CARRY

travel lighter

As you walk your path and live each beautiful day, only carry the things with you that make you feel lighter. Carry the things that make each day just a little bit lighter— a little bit easier. Carry the things that add a little bit more magic and wonder. My beautiful friend, always carry hope with you. Every single day, hold onto relentless hope for brighter days and unexpected miracles— hope that no matter what today looked like, tomorrow can be even brighter. And with hope in your heart, carry joy wherever you are. Know that your smile has the power to make even the greyest day shine so bright. It holds the power to turn a bad day into an alright one and an alright one into an extraordinary day. Always carry bravery with you. Bravery to face your obstacles and overcome the challenges thrown at you. Bravery to let your true self be seen, no matter who is watching. My beautiful friend, as you go, keep your mind and heart wide open. Keep your mind open to learning and growing and seeing everything that is out there. Keep your heart open to feel all of the love that is out there that is meant just for you. Carry the things that make each day lighter, my beautiful friend. It will make all the difference.

Only carry the things that make you feel light,
the things that make you feel free.

Let go of any doubts, you can do it.
Let go of any fears, it really will be okay.
Let go of any pressure, you got this.

letting go

Let go of everything that is weighing you down. Set down the heavy weight of fears and doubts, pains and old wounds. My beautiful friend, you are not meant to carry that heaviness with you every day. Like a heavy bag hanging on your back, it only brings your shoulders and head down. Each step becomes much harder, making moving forward an enormous task instead of just a little step ahead. The doubts about yourself and your capabilities are too heavy, my beautiful friend. You are so wonderfully capable. The potential just flows out of you for all of the things you can do. It does not matter what anyone else has told you. It does not matter what things you have tried and failed at before. *Period.* You are alive and breathing; you are capable of growing and becoming and changing however you would like. Set down your fears of things not working out. Maybe it won't work out, but maybe it will. And either way, everything is okay just as it is now. Later will come and you will be able to find joy and love no matter how it all works out. So let your fear go and focus just on this day and what you can do now. Set down all of the things you were never meant to hold, my beautiful friend. You are meant to hold so many beautiful things; but heaviness is not one of them.

with hope in your heart

No matter what mountain you are climbing or what valley you are navigating through, hold onto hope, my beautiful friend. Hold onto hope in the good times and the bad, on the days of sunny skies and the days of endless rain. Replace your fears with boundless, relentless courage. Drown out your doubts with an overflow of hope for all of the good things are coming. Let hope light your path when all you can see is darkness. Let hope create joy out of the times where there seems to be none... Hope is feeling heavy raindrops crashing onto your skin, but still smiling about the incredible light that is coming after the storm. It is feeling the immense pain of heartbreak but knowing that there is still boundless love in the world meant for you. It is knowing that today might hold everything you have been waiting so long for. Hope is not just a little word to toss around lightly. *No.* Hope is a powerful seed that you plant in your heart knowing without a doubt that in time, it will bloom into a magnificent garden. Hope has the power to bring the bright sun of tomorrow into today. Always carry hope in your heart, my beautiful friend because sometimes, hope will be the thing that carries *you.*

Fill your heart
with so much hope
it overflows.

If only you could see
just how bright your smile is.
Oh my sweet friend,
how bright it lights up the room.

your bright smile

When you smile, you light up your day and the day of those around you. Your smile sends a signal to your heart letting it know you are okay, and in return, you really do become happier. Your smile lets your heart know that you are still looking for the rainbows during the rain and that you are still looking for the blessings instead of dwelling in pain.

Some days, it is easy to smile. The sun is out, you are going out with your friends, you just got a promotion. You have the entire world in your hands! But on the days that it is harder, instead of waiting for something out there to make you smile, learn how to bring out your smile from within. If blasting your favorite singer or band while taking a walk always brings a smile to your face, spend a few minutes walking with your music every single day. If watching your favorite comedian online makes you laugh every time, watch them every single morning to start your day in good spirits. If you have a favorite book or podcast that you always enjoy, read or listen to it whenever you have a free moment. My sweet friend, whatever it takes to bring a beautiful and genuine smile to your face— a smile that crinkles the corner of your eyes and lights you from the inside out— do that as often as you possibly can. Life is too precious to go through it without your smile.

a determined heart pt. 1

When I write, *believe in yourself,* my beautiful friend, *this* is what I mean: I mean that you should believe wholeheartedly in who you are. You should believe that you are wonderful and beautiful and capable and incredible and amazing. *Because you are.* It does not matter how you did in school, it does not matter what job you have or do not have. It does not matter what your past looked like or who you were before. None of those things matter. What matters is that you believe in who you are right now in this moment. That you believe that despite it all, you are still overflowing with beauty and wonder and capability and possibility for your future. When I write, *believe in yourself,* I mean that you should believe that you have worlds inside of you waiting to come out into the real world. You have unique dreams planted as seeds inside of you waiting to come to life. You have incredible ideas patiently waiting to become reality. I mean that you should believe in those seeds of dreams and ideas and wishes because the world wants them— the world needs the uniqueness that you bring. I mean that you should believe in yourself regardless of your doubts. When I write, *believe in yourself,* I mean that even if the odds are against you a million to one, that you still bet on yourself. *Every single time.*

a determined heart pt. 2

Your determined heart will take you so far, my beautiful friend. It will take you to peaks so high and oceans so vast that you never could have dreamed them up. It is stronger than any doubts, any fears, any uncertainty. Your determined heart knows that what can be seen is deceiving— it knows that to make the future that you dream of come to life, you have to see what is not yet here. *Trust your determined heart*, my beautiful friend. It beats so strong and faithfully inside of you, *always*. It is full of restless passion and incredible boldness, relentless effort and unwavering persistence. Your determined heart is what will turn your dreams into reality and your falls into opportunities. It will not just open doors for you, but it will show you doors that you would have never seen otherwise. When your legs are weary and your feet are tired, your determined heart will carry you through. And with your determined heart, nothing in the world will ever be able to stop you. *Nothing*.

summoning courage

There is boundless bravery and courage within you, my sweet friend. *Summon it.* Being brave is knowing that things might not work out, but giving your all anyways. Being brave is choosing to be strong when you feel your weakest. Being brave is about daring to keep pushing your limits further and further. It is about shattering the ceiling you thought was keeping you down, and then realizing not only is there no ceiling, but that you have wings too and there is no limit to the places that you can go. You hold so much bravery in your heart that you have never even seen before, my sweet friend. You become brave by *being* brave. You become brave by trusting in yourself and taking the leap. You become brave by pushing your edges a little bit further every day. By extending those wings just a little bit more each time. It is already within you, my sweet friend. You already have your wings to soar.

Do it.
Shatter the ceiling.
Break the mold.
Destroy the chains.
Do all of the things
you thought you couldn't do.

This is just one stepping stone
towards the life that's ahead for you.

where you need to be

Always, *always* hold on tightly to faith that you are right where you need to be. Hold onto faith in yourself and your journey. Hold onto faith that it will unfold in all of the ways that it is meant to. Faith is knowing that where you are now does not determine all of the places that you will go. It is knowing that this is just a stepping stone on your beautiful path. Faith is knowing that there are so many things working for you far beyond what you can see that are building your path. And it is being okay with not needing to understand it all. Faith is choosing to trust in those things that you cannot see. Trusting that the things that go wrong are steering you towards what is right. Trusting that what you have been waiting and working for is right around the corner. Trusting that each step you take is helping you on your way. Hold onto your faith in every season, my sweet friend. *You are on your way.*

openness

Keep your mind and heart wide open to experience everything that this life has in store for you. Stay open to experience it fully and deeply and entirely. Let yourself fall into the love and wonder and magic of being alive. Keep your mind open to learning and expanding and growing in new ways. Keep your mind open to discovering and becoming, even if it is uncomfortable to step into the new. Keep your heart open to living. There is so much out there for you to see and experience and do. So much that you cannot even fathom. People that will change your life. Love that will fill your heart like you have never felt before. Jobs that will fill your soul with purpose and meaning. There is so much out there for you, stay open to receiving it all, my beautiful friend.

Keep your eyes wide,
your heart open,
and your soul free.

3. YOUR GUIDE

intuition

Trust that your heart will always lead you in the right direction towards all of the things that are meant for you. My beautiful friend, your heart often knows things before your mind does. It knows if you are headed in the right direction or if that person is meant for you. It knows if you need to walk away or if you need to try something new. It can see and understand things before you can put it into words. Your heart speaks in those feelings deep within you. It is that feeling when you are drawn to someone or something and it just feels so *right* inside— like coming home, like being with that person that your walls can just come down when you are around, like knowing that you are right where you belong. And it is that feeling when things just feel *off* too — like walking into a place where it just feels wrong, like being with someone that you have to try so hard to be around... My beautiful friend, trust that your heart knows what is best for you. Trust those feelings deep inside about people and situations. Trust that there is a reason even when you cannot see.

When the storms are raging around you,
learn to calm the waters within.

turbulent waters

It is not always easy to hear your heart, my sweet friend. Sometimes the water becomes wild and turbulent, not letting you see what is going on beneath the surface. When you are overwhelmed with tasks and checklists and a full calendar, rampant waves can start to form within. When you are hurt or frustrated or broken, the water swells and falls with your deep emotions. When you are battling between who you truly are and who you think you should be— when you are trying too hard to be someone you are not— the storms rage within. My sweet friend, waves will always come into your life. There will always be a lot going on around you. So learn to calm the waters within. Maybe you will not ever be able to solve everything going on out there, but you can create peaceful waters within. Distance yourself from everything causing the storms. Take a break from the people that are causing the pushes and pulls within you. Leave the situations that are tugging at you. Allow your body to truly rest. Take deep breaths and return to the steady beat of your heart. Let the waves settle. Remind yourself that you are safe. That you are okay. And then, with steady waters, allow your heart to guide you back home.

deep roots

My beautiful friend, never forget how deep your roots run. The life that runs through all of the tallest oaks and the most vibrant roses runs through you. The energy that pushes and pulls the tides and moves the earth and the moon, flows through *you*. The roots you have run so deep, my beautiful friend. You are a part of this world. You make a difference in this world. All of the things you do and the interactions you make leave a ripple on everyone around you. You are enough as you are, my beautiful friend. Being you just how you are is how we need you. It is how the world needs you. You belong here as much as the golden sun and the shining stars and the palm trees and the butterflies. You are a piece of this world. Your roots run as deep as the universe itself. And with your deep roots, you can go as far as your dreams take you.

Nikki Banas

ground yourself

Along your beautiful and winding journey, never go too far without taking a few moments to ground yourself and reconnect with your core, my beautiful friend. Take a few moments as often as you can to ground yourself— to reconnect with your roots. Use these moments to remind yourself that you are a beautiful part of this world and that the world would not be the same without you and everything that you give. Take just a few moments to remind yourself where you are now and remember where you have already been. And ground yourself in knowing that you are so wonderfully capable and strong. More than you could ever know. Never go too far without grounding yourself, my beautiful friend. Never go too long without taking a few moments just for you.

46

becoming you

Become the person that you want to be. Do not become who others think you should be. Do not become someone who holds your true spirit tucked and folded inside because you think it is too much or too loud or too different for the world out there. My sweet friend, become exactly who you want to become. Become who *you* dream of becoming. Become someone you will be so proud of when you look back on you. Become someone you love inside and out simply because you are *you*. Because my sweet friend, you are so incredibly unique. You are so worthy and wonderful and beautiful and strong. You are capable and more than enough. And when you are yourself, you attract all of the things and people that are meant to be with you too. You attract those who see you just as you are and that light your soul from the inside out. You attract the things that make your life endlessly beautiful and wonderful and soulful. You attract everything that is meant to be yours.

If you could become anyone,
who would you choose to become?

your heart

You are meant for boundless love. You are meant for smiles so big and true, that wrinkles form around your lips. Laughs so hard your belly aches. Love so passionate you soar. Your heart knows that you are meant to live— and not just to live— but to live deeply and fully and entirely. Your heart knows that you are meant to experience everything in this life that is meant just for you. And if you let it, your heart will guide you towards all of it. It won't be all sunshine and good times. It won't be all smiles and things gone perfectly. *Not at all.* It will be messy. There will be really hard times but there will also be times full of so much joy and light that you will feel like you are on top of the whole entire world. That nothing at all can stop you... Your heart will guide you through the darkest nights to teach you that all of the light you could ever need is already within you. It will guide you through the toughest droughts to show you that you really can make it through the hardest times. It will guide you through unfair obstacles and challenges to prove to you that you are so strong and capable and that you need to believe it too. Your heart will guide you through it all. It will guide you towards everything you are meant for. It won't always be easy, but my beautiful friend, it *will always* be worth it.

build yourself up

Build yourself up, my sweet friend. Build yourself up like you would your best friend or your own child. Build yourself up like you would someone you love boundlessly and unconditionally. Build yourself up how you are *meant* to be built up. Turn the wishes tucked in your heart into goals and plans and then bring them to life with little steps every day. Cheer for yourself with each step you take. Root for yourself regardless of if anyone else is or not. Root for yourself after you stand up after stumbling and when you reach a new height. Believe in yourself unconditionally. Believe in yourself like you know with absolute certainty that you will get there. Commit to growing and expanding and pouring into yourself because my sweet friend, you deserve your unconditional love too.

Become one of the people who
completely,
entirely,
without a doubt,
believes in **you**
and all that you will become.

Because my sweet friend,
you are capable of every
dream that enters your heart.

4. HERE

Whenever you doubt how far you can go,
just look at how far you've come.

how far you've come

Whether you are where you want to be or not, my sweet friend, be proud of how far you've already come. You've gone through *so much* to get here. You've gone through so many dark winters and beautiful summers. You kept going when all you wanted to do was give up. You've come a long way, my sweet friend. Be proud of the person you've become. Be proud of how many mountains you've already conquered and how far you've already climbed. Find peace in the path that led you here, regardless of how difficult it was. Know that that path is behind you and that there is a beautiful and unexplored path ahead of you still. Find peace in everything you've been through— know that every battle you've faced and battle you've survived has helped shape who you are now. Find peace in knowing that even with all you've already gone through, there is still so much ahead for you. There are new horizons for you, my sweet friend. There are still so many life-changing opportunities and beautiful memories to be made. So let the path behind you inspire your path ahead. Let the growth you've already had remind you that there is still boundless growth ahead. Be proud of the path you've taken to get here, even with all of its bumps and turns, because it led you here. And from here, your path is only bound by your imagination, my sweet friend.

a letter to her

Thank your past self for everything she has done for you, my sweet friend. Thank her for everything she did to get you here. Thank her for the lessons she learned, especially the ones she had to learn the hard way, because you learned so much from them. Thank her for all of the times she could have easily just thrown in the towel and given up, but she dug her heels in and kept on going anyway. Thank her for all of the mistakes she made because it meant that she kept on trying. Thank her for the mountains she climbed to get you here, for the battles she fought and for all of the tough choices she had to make. Thank her for the bridges she built and climbed over and the bridges she burned to the ground. She might not have done everything perfectly— and she might have done everything *wildly* far from perfect— but she did her best with what she had. She tried. She gave so much. She gave so much for you. Forgive her for her mistakes and failures, my sweet friend, and love her entirely because it is only because of her that you are so wonderfully *you* now.

greatest teacher

Our paths behind us are our greatest teachers. The mountains we climbed taught us a lot about the mountains themselves, but more so, they taught us about *us*. They taught us that if we are determined, there is no mountain that is too tall for us to climb. The hardships we endured taught us that we are made of grit and fire and strength and courage. They taught us that sometimes the only way to truly understand our strength is to put us under so much pressure that we have no other choice. The storms we faced taught us that no matter how thunderous the clouds, no matter how long the rain pours, the sun comes back. *Always*. They taught us that not all storms will give us time to prepare. Some will come roaring and unannounced. They taught us that sometimes all we can do is hold on tight and endure, but that eventually we *will* make it through. And the best times we savored taught us what we are truly meant for in our lives— that we are meant for good and light and joy and laughter and moments that feel like magic. They taught us that there are so many beautiful memories to be made and laughs to be shared.

your power

No matter how tough it was, no matter what you have seen on your way here, no matter how badly you wish you could change it, your past is a part of you. But my sweet friend, you get to choose which parts of it you will give power to. You can give power to all of the times you fell *or* you can give power to all of the times you rose. You can give power to the times you messed up, failed, and made mistakes or you can give power to all of the times that you tried, gave your best, and did what you could. You can think about the bad times over and over and over, or my sweet friend, you can give them *not one more drop* of your power and you can think about all of the good times. All of the beautiful moments. All of the times you rose. You can give your energy to celebrating the good. You can pour your heart into being proud that despite it all, you made it here. You can choose to let go of the things simply because they are too heavy and taking too much of your power. My sweet friend, give your precious energy and power to the things that deserve your power. *And not one more drop to the things that don't.*

Your past has helped shape who you are
but it does not define who you can be.

this moment

Embrace the beauty and wonder of this precious little moment—there is so much here just for you, my beautiful friend. There is light tucked in the corners all around you just waiting for you to discover it. There is magic in this little moment. There are endless possibilities for what you can do. There is life flowing through you and extending out into the world all around you. Embrace this beautiful moment for all that it is. Embrace who you are right now entirely. Embrace both the things you love about yourself and the things that you wish you could change most. Embrace it all because it is all *you*. Embrace the challenges you are facing right now. They mean that you are striving and growing. Set down yesterday and do not pick up tomorrow yet, and instead, embrace everything already here for you, today.

acceptance and love

Everything is okay, just as it is now. I promise you. My sweet friend, you are alive and breathing and so strong. Your heart is beating and well, and your breath is steady and strong. You've conquered entire mountains and you have walked through the darkest nights. You might not be where you want to be right now, but you are on your way. Do not compare where you are to where anyone else is— your journey is so wildly your own that there is not one single reason it should look like anyone else's. And do not compare where you are to where you think you should have been by now. There is nowhere else you should be right now. If you were meant to be elsewhere, I promise you would be there, my sweet friend. There is so much here in this moment— exactly where you are now— for you. Accept here. Be here— be here *entirely*. Be here knowing that you are on your way, and that *that* is enough. Let go of thinking you should be elsewhere and pour that energy into looking at everything that is around you now... Everything is okay, just how it is now. There are still worlds ahead for you. There is still boundless light ahead. My sweet friend, this is just the beginning.

Oh my beautiful friend,
if only you could see how this will all unfold.
Even after everything,
there is still so much ahead for you.

yet to come

There is so much for you up ahead that you can't even imagine yet, my beautiful friend. The hard times you are facing? They are *not* permanent. *Not at all.* They are not here to stay. These moments are not your entire story. Not even close. Better times are around the corner— you just can't see them quite yet. Things are changing and working to turn in your favor. You will heal from this. You will overcome this challenge. You will find the peace you have been looking so long for. You will find new strength and new light that you didn't know existed within you. You will grow and rise out of these times. *You will.* And the good times you are facing? Oh, my beautiful friend you haven't even begun to experience the good... Oh no, *not at all.* This is nothing compared to how much good and love and joy and light is up ahead. You are just dancing in the shallow end of the depth of joy that is coming. There are people you have not met yet that are going to light up your entire world. Opportunities that you never thought were possible will come to you. Moments ahead full of so much magic that you will swear you are living a scene from a movie. There are still so many beautiful horizons ahead for you, my beautiful friend. The best is still yet to come.

keep looking up

Always keep looking up, my beautiful friend. Keep looking up at the sky when all you want to do is keep your eyes on the ground. Let its ever changing colors and textures remind you that everything changes and moves in time. Let it show you that wherever you are, you are not stuck there. Let its vastness remind you that you live in a big, beautiful, infinite world and that there is still so much for you to see and discover out there. Let the rhythm of the sun and the moon ground you with their patters and remind you that we all go through ups and downs. We all go through phases and cycles, but in time we always return to full. Let the night sky remind you that beautiful shining stars can only be seen in the darkness. And let the daytime sky remind you that like the clouds always float away, your troubles always will too. My beautiful friend, know that there is so much more out there just for you. And if you ever need a reminder, remember to keep looking up.

Along the Way

Like the sun and all of the stars,
you are meant to shine.

5. THE FOOT OF THE MOUNTAIN

a new chapter

You cannot have a new beginning without an ending first. And you cannot have an ending without a new beginning that follows. Endings and beginnings exist together, my beautiful friend. In order to grow into who you are meant to become, you have to be willing to let go of pieces of your old self. And not only do you have to be willing to let go of the old, but you have to be willing to let go of it *before* you can see the new— before you can see the incredible bloom that is ahead. Before you can see all of the beautiful moments that lie ahead. You have to let go of the old with trust of the new. My beautiful friend, you have to stop pouring your precious energy into the things that are no longer serving you. You have to begin pouring into the new... You have to pour into the things that you want to see grow. Like an oak in the fall, let go of your weathered leaves. There is no use holding on to them— they served their purpose and now they are only in the way of growing the new. You will lose the things you know. You will lose this routine and piece of you that you have been working so long for. But when this season comes to an end, always remember that it means a new season is coming. A new beginning is coming. A new chapter with so many delightful and unimaginable things that you cannot imagine yet. Shift into the new. Shift into the possibilities and wonder ahead. It is ready for you.

During every ending—
no matter how heartbreaking or
unexpected or difficult—
hold on tight to the beginning that is ahead.

begin again

Whenever you would like, you can begin again. It is never too late or too early to start steering your life in a new direction towards a different shore. Whenever you want or need, my sweet friend, you can begin again. It does not matter how long you have been traveling this road that you are on, if you want to steer into something new, you can. It is never too late. You are never too far into something that you cannot turn around. *Never.* It does not matter how much you have poured yourself and everything you could into this path. If this is not the way for you anymore— if your relationship is just not working, if your job is just not right, if your home does not feel like home anymore, if your friends are bringing you down or hurting you— you can walk away. You can turn in a brand new direction. If this is not the way, my sweet friend, walk away. Begin again. Begin finding your way towards everything that is meant for you. Begin letting your old story go so that you can step into all the new that is waiting for you.

the unknown

New paths are made of the unknown, my beautiful friend. And the unknown is made of uncertainty and risk and doubts. It holds many questions with very few answers... But the unknown also holds excitement for its endless possibilities. It holds hope for all of the good things that could come and the dreams that could come to life. So maybe things will not work out, but my beautiful friend, *maybe they will*. Maybe this will be the journey you never knew you needed. The one that shows you just how incredible and beautiful and breathtaking you are. Maybe this is the one that touches your heart and soul. The one that changes you forever. Maybe this is the one that shows you that it is okay to leave your past behind you. The one that shows you that there is still boundless life ahead for you. Maybe this is the one that changes how you *live*. The one that lights you up from the inside out with a light so bright that nothing could ever dim its shine. So maybe you are walking into the unknown. My beautiful friend, walk with your head held so high because this unknown? This unknown just might hold everything you have been waiting your whole life for.

spread your wings...

You are ready for what is next. You are strong enough, capable enough, smart enough. You can tackle whatever obstacles come to you and can overcome every challenge. My beautiful friend, if you have any doubts, *look*. Look back at how far you have already come. Look at how much you have already grown and everything you have conquered. Look at how much you have already grown. Look back to remind yourself that you are ready for everything ahead. It might be easier to stay with what you have known for so long. It might be easier to stay at shore where it's safe. But that is not where *life* happens. Life happens when you set sail. Life happens when you *jump*. It happens when you spread your wings so wide and allow yourself to soar. Life happens when you leave the shore to see what is really out there for you. You are ready. You are capable and strong. Trust your wings, my beautiful friend. You are ready.

...and jump

It can be the hardest thing in the world to do: to be afraid and to still jump. To have absolutely no idea what will happen after your feet leave the ground but to still take the leap. My sweet friend, you can be afraid. You are perfectly allowed to be afraid of the unknown, the deep waters, the uncertainty, the risk. You are perfectly allowed to be afraid and hesitant and unsure and doubtful. *You are human.* But please, *please*, never let being afraid stop you from all of the beautiful things that life has in store for you. Never let your fear stop you from trying all of the things that your soul begs you to do. Never let it stop you from trusting your heart. There is so much out there for you on the other side of fear. There is so much that you cannot possibly imagine, my sweet friend. Places you cannot even imagine. Cities and cultures and foods that you have never heard of. People who will turn your entire world upside down. Souls that will make you see your world in a whole new way. Do not wait to feel completely ready. Do not wait until you are entirely sure of yourself. Do not wait until you feel like you are enough. If you have the idea tucked within your mind, *try it*. If your heart is telling you to get out there, *get out there*. If your soul yearns for something more, *go in search of something more*. If deep inside you want to make a jump— regardless of how small or how large— do it. My sweet friend, jump. And when you jump, you might just find that your wings have been waiting within you the entire time.

Nikki Banas

canvas

My beautiful friend, you came into this world a blank canvas just waiting to be filled. You came knowing very little— you came in not knowing how to stand up or to say a word, not knowing the difference between up and down or left and right. You came into this life full of potential just overflowing from within you and the brush in your hand. My beautiful friend, you *still* hold this incredible canvas just waiting to be filled. Even after everything you have been through and everything you have learned, even after all of the ways you have already grown so much, you still get to paint your canvas however you would like. You can paint over everything you have known and start a brand new painting. You can add new details or change the old ones. Even after everything, you *still* hold the paint and the brush, my beautiful friend. It is never too late or too early to start painting the picture you want to see for your life. It is never too late or too early to begin again or to change it all. The brush is entirely yours.

wildly capable

You are so wildly capable, my sweet friend. Even if others have told you otherwise, even if you have thought differently, you are still *so* wildly capable. You have so much potential inside of you that is just waiting to burst out into this world. You have so many unique ideas that are meant to come to life. You have countless dreams that are meant to come true. My sweet friend, you have so much within you that you cannot see. And even when you cannot see it or feel it, it is there. It fills every fiber of your being. It fills your heart and runs through every vein in your body. My sweet friend, you are limitless. There are no bounds to what you can do besides the ones you create for yourself. Others may put you in a box, but there is no box. There is no ceiling. The sky is not even your limit, my sweet friend— there simply are none. So let your wings spread as wide as you can and then allow yourself to soar.

6. THE CLIMB

your own pace

My sweet friend, take your time as you go. Do not rush your climb. Do not rush to get through another day or to reach the next milestone. Do not rush to get there as fast as you can. *There is no rush.* So my sweet friend, like the sun decides its pace to rise and set and the leaves decide their pace to bloom and fall, decide your own pace for life. Decide the pace that fits *you* because there is no rush to your growth. There is no rush for your bloom. You are growing and becoming in your own time and in your own way. Your growth will not look like anyone else's and that is how it is supposed to be. You are not supposed to be further along or have already done all of those things by this age. Like we do not rush the lilies to bloom into their magnificent colors each spring, do not rush yourself to grow either. Trust that you are absorbing what you need each day to grow and flourish. Know that you are growing within if you cannot see it outside of you yet. My sweet friend, grow at your own pace.

Along the Way

Like the sun and the moon decide
their pace to rise and fall,
you get to decide your own pace for it all.

Nikki Banas

commit

You have to commit to yourself, my beautiful friend. I mean it. You have to commit to yourself and everything you deserve from this life. You have to show up for yourself, both when it is easy and when it is hard. You have to show up for yourself regardless of who else out there shows up for you. You have to accept yourself on your best and your worst days. Even when you are frustrated and angry with yourself. Even when you have made so many mistakes and feel like you are so stuck. You've got to accept yourself anyways, my beautiful friend. You have to believe in yourself even when no one else does. You have to cheer for yourself and celebrate all of your victories because I promise you that you are doing so many things worth celebrating. You have to set your own goals and work on yourself. Not for anyone out there, but because you deserve to become the best version of yourself. You've got to respect and take care of your mind and body. You've got to nourish your heart and soul. Because before you can ever go and do anything out in the world, you have to take care of your own world within. And my beautiful friend, *you are worth committing to.*

Along the Way

resistance

My sweet friend, never let resistance keep you from trying. Never let it stop you from getting to where you are meant to go. Resistance only comes when you are close to something bigger and something greater. It comes when you are close to that new height and better place ahead. It comes when something so wonderful is right around the corner. My beautiful friend, resistance comes when you are trying something new and you have to stretch yourself to reach that new height. It is in those moments of stretch when resistance says that you cannot do it. It says that you are reaching too high and that you should go back into your comfort zone. My sweet friend, do not listen. You can do it, *period*. You can. You can stretch yourself to reach that new height. Never let it keep you from trying because the moments of greatest resistance hold the greatest reward on the other side. And when you do keep going despite the resistance— when you keep trying anyway— you are showing the universe that you will not back down. That that goal, that dream, that milestone is *yours*, and that you will not stop until it is in your hands. Whether it comes from your own fears or doubts, from others around you, from the situations you are in, you can overcome it. Allow yourself to see it and acknowledge that you are feeling resistance to what you are trying to do and then, continue forward anyway. You can feel the pull and still push forward. Because what's on the other side? *It's always worth it.*

Do not wait for courage to continue,
choose to be courageous and continue anyway.

bloom

My sweet friend, you already have everything you need inside of you. You already have the courage to get through this challenge. You already have the capabilities to win this battle. You already have the heart to see this through. It's all inside of you. Like a seed holds everything it needs to become a beautiful, grand oak, you hold everything inside of you to become the greatest version of you. You have what you need to overcome these obstacles. You have what you need to grow. Nourish and believe in yourself, my sweet friend. Everything you need is within you.

progress

Every day does not need to be perfect. Every day does not need to be a new success, a grand victory, or a new peak. You by no means need to solve everything today. And trying to do so can leave you overwhelmed and exhausted. My beautiful friend, you do not need to do everything today. You just need to take one step ahead in the right direction. Put one more little piece of the puzzle into place. Add one little thing that will make today a better day than yesterday. Sometimes it's easy to forget the value of just one small step, but one step in the right direction has the power to change everything. When it comes down to it, it's not about making this day perfect at all. It's about doing your best today with what you have. Because life throws curveballs. The unexpected happens. The expected doesn't happen. Things do not always go how we thought. So when you feel like you are off track, like you have already failed, or like you are already too far behind, my beautiful friend, just take one step in the right direction. Not one hundred. Not ten. But one. Slow it down, take a breath, and take that one step ahead. Because more times than not, that's really all it takes.

giving your best

My sweet friend, it is okay if your best looks different each day. Some days you will find inspiration and motivation in everything around you. It will be easy to give your entire self to the people around you and the projects that you are working on. But some days, you will try and try, and just find it so difficult to give anything your full attention. It will feel like trudging through mud just to get done a fraction of what you normally can. My sweet friend, you are human. You are not a machine who can give full power every day of the week and month. You need time to rest and recharge— time to simply *be*. Give your best with what you can every day, but know that it will ebb and flow too. Like phases of the moon and the cycles of the sun, you are not always in the same phase. It takes time to return to full, but you will get there.

eyes ahead

No matter what, my sweet friend, keep your eyes ahead. *Always ahead.* Keep your eyes focused on everything that you are working so hard for and keep your heart set towards where you want to go. Keep giving it your all every single day and pushing yourself even further. Others might say that you are wasting your time or that what you are doing is impossible. They might tell you how they think you should be spending your time and efforts. My beautiful friend, do not listen. Hear them, but then politely walk away. They do not know you and what you are made of— they have no idea what dreams lay within your heart. So when others are trying to bring you down, look inward. Remind yourself that you are meant for greatness. You are meant to soar to incredible heights and do incredible things. You were born with wings to soar— not to stay planted on the ground. Know that where you are going is worth every single step— no matter how difficult. My beautiful friend, there is so much ahead for you, so keep your heart pointing forward and your eyes on where you are going. You *will* get there.

If only you could see the joy
the passion
the presence
the love—
the life—
that awaits you.

who you are

To the ones who treat you badly for no reason, the ones who hurt you without an apology, the ones who drag you down, my sweet friend, let them go. Let go of their harsh words and move on. Do not take their words personally or continue repeating them in your head. Do not carry their heavy weight... My sweet friend, only you get to define you. *Only you.* Their lack of love does not mean that you do not deserve love. Their lack of kindness does not mean that you do not deserve kindness. You are deserving of joy and love and kindness. What they say and how they act has nothing to do with you— and everything to do with them. Let their words roll off your back and keep climbing on. Your time is too precious to spend trying to please everyone or get on everyone's good side. It is an impossible task anyway and you have bigger— *so much* bigger— things to do and focus on. So let their words go, remind yourself that you are incredibly worthy and wonderful and beautiful, and then continue on.

You have much more important things to do
with your one unique, boundless, incredible life,
than to try and appease the unappeasable.

set sail

Never be afraid to seek out a new horizon, my sweet friend. Never be afraid to leave your comfort zone to expand even further... There is so much out there for you — so much so that it is impossible to imagine all that is there for you. There are endless new horizons out there for you to experience and discover but you cannot get there without leaving the shore *here*. You cannot sail into beautiful new waters without leaving the ones you have always known. Growth is about reinventing yourself, it is about continually evolving and expanding yourself. It's about sailing for new horizons that force you to stretch and reach into the unknown. It's about trying the things that you think you cannot do— and learning that you really can do them. Growth is about thinking beyond what you have always known and daring to go even further. There is so much out there for you, my sweet friend. *It is time to set sail.*

fear

Fear will undoubtedly join you on your journey. Do not try to shut it away or ignore it. Instead, *let it in*. Let yourself feel your fear, whether it is fear of not being good enough, fear of failing, or fear of falling apart. Do not try to pretend it is not there or force it out, feel it. That fear means that you are pushing yourself further. That yes, you are headed into a little bit of the unknown but that you are pushing. That fear means that you are doing something outside of your comfort zone and that you are putting yourself out there, looking for something *more*, something bigger and greater. So let it in. Let it in as a reminder that you are growing and expanding. And my beautiful friend, know that whenever fear is with you, so is courage. They travel with you together, and you get to decide which to give power to. Fear may be beside you, tugging at you telling you to step back and take it easy. But courage is right there too, embracing you for the big step ahead of you, knowing that you have what it takes. You can feel your fear without giving it all of your power. You can acknowledge it, feel it, and then let it go to hold on to courage. Fear may come along for the ride, but my beautiful friend, always let courage be your guide.

Sometimes you just need to stop thinking
and just do the thing... Make the call, start the project,
give the apology, try something new.

doing

A lot of things are much easier and simpler and less scary than we think. Things in our mind sometimes amplify— raindrops turn into hurricanes and darkness turns into nightmares. Tasks turn into projects and checklists turn into anxiety... But the only way to conquer them is to have courage and just do them. To just start doing *something*, to begin and try. And oftentimes, in finally starting those things, you realize that it was never really as bad as you thought it would be. That the task you have been putting off really wasn't that bad at all. That the phone call you had to make only took a few moments. And the more you stop your thoughts and just begin, the more you will find that you are so much stronger and more capable than you realized. That you can handle so many things so well. And sometimes, in doing those things, you will find that it really is fun to do what you thought you couldn't.

Nikki Banas

true strength

Your true strength comes from within you, my beautiful friend. Your true strength comes from how you keep showing up every single day— even after everything you've been through and every battle you've faced. Your true strength comes from how you keep giving it your all — even when you don't know if it will be enough. It comes from how you keep trying— even after making mistakes or failing... My beautiful friend, know that you have so much more strength inside of you than you realize too. You have the strength to climb the tallest mountains, you have the strength to overcome the toughest hurdles. You have the strength to get through any darkness that comes your way. It's all within you.

Choose to believe in your strength
even when you feel at your weakest.

rest

When you are tired from walking, when your soul is heavy from weeks or months or years of exhaustion, when your heart wants to give up, my sweet friend, *rest*. Put on the most comfortable clothes you own, lay down under the softest and warmest blankets, and allow yourself to rest. Tuck away the to-do list, hide every missed email and call, and let yourself simply breathe. You have gone through so much. You have been working so hard and have been carrying the weight of so much more than you were ever meant to carry. *So rest.* Set down the heaviness. Let your shoulders fall and your jaw relax. Let the tension out of your muscles. You are still so beautiful. You still hold endless light inside of you. Your eyes may be tired, but they still shine so bright. Your heart may be weary or broken, but it is still beating so strong. Your soul may ache, but it is still so full of life. So when you are overworked, when you are exhausted, when you cannot push any further, my sweet friend, *rest*.

like the rings of a tree

No season of growth will look the same, my beautiful friend, and that is okay. Every season is not meant to look the same. Like the rings of a tree, each season of growth is different from the last. And that is what makes each season so beautiful. Some seasons hold the perfect conditions. They have the right amount of light and plenty of water. They have great air quality and little wind. But other rings show the reckless storms they endured. The long droughts. The burning and healing from forest fires. And through it all, they still grow. They still continue to expand and spread their branches. They still allow their leaves to bloom... And wherever you are — if you are in a season of drought or a season of perfect conditions— know that you can find growth right where you are. This season might not have the perfect conditions— and it might be far from them— but do not wait for the conditions to become perfect to build yourself. You can still grow here. You can still use the storms to become stronger. You can still find joy here. You can still create love right where you are. No matter what season you are in, my beautiful friend, you are still growing.

And never forget that
you are becoming even more you,
with every moment,
with every breath.

becoming

You never really finish becoming. Becoming is less about a bloom and more about the growth. It is about growing and changing as your life evolves and shifts with the seasons. It is about learning to become a little softer, a little kinder, and a little more gentle in order to ride the waves that life undoubtedly brings. It is about learning to give your best with what you've got right here, in this moment right now. And it is about being okay with that too. It is about being a little bit more you each day— trying new hobbies or styles, following your gut a little bit more, trusting your heart even when you are nervous. It is about growing in ways that you never knew you could. Becoming is not about getting to a distant place that holds joy and magic and light, it is about realizing that there is joy and magic and light to be found as you grow *along the way*.

7. A BREAK BY THE WATER

pause

Look at the world around you right now, my sweet friend. Pause and take it all in wherever you are as you read these words— if you are tucked in a blanket on your couch on a cozy winter's day, or if you are at a local café surrounded by hustling people going about their busy days. If you are in a quiet, old library surrounded by thousands and thousands of beautiful books just waiting to be read, or if you are out on your porch with only the delicate songs of birds filling the air. Whether everything else in your life is going smoothly or a bit rocky, whether these are the first quiet moments you have had in a long time or you find quiet moments for yourself each day, allow yourself to pause completely in this moment. Allow yourself to *really* feel this moment— everything you can see and feel and hear and taste. Write everything you feel on this page if you would like— make this moment permanent. Allow yourself to take a step away from every moment behind you and do not think of any moment to come. Instead, allow yourself to completely savor this one and everything it brings. Let its peace and beauty and joy fill every corner of your being, my sweet friend. Allow yourself to feel it all.

Allow yourself to savor
this beautiful little moment of now.

alive & breathing

It is truly a beautiful, wonderful, and incredible thing to just be here. To have the sight to be able to read these words right now. To be able to move our bodies and stretch our minds. To be able to sing and dance and love. To have people to love and people that love us. To be a part of what is so much bigger than ourselves. The world we live in is infinite and extends deeper, further, and wider than we could ever imagine. There is no limit to what we can learn or become or do or create. There is no limit to the places we can explore and the sights we can see. There are more possibilities than we could ever imagine for our lives. It is truly a precious gift to be here, alive and breathing. There are so many beautiful things to be thankful for every day. Everything may not be perfect— and may be far from it— but things do not need to be perfect to still be boundlessly beautiful.

Let things be imperfectly beautiful
just as they are.

There is so much magic
just for you
in this very moment.

slowing down

When your world is spinning too quickly and everything around you is moving too fast, my sweet friend, *slow – it – down*. Take however much time you need just for you. Time to re-center and reconnect with your beautiful spirit. Take time to check in with how you are *really* doing inside. Are you happy? Are you burned out? Do you feel joy in your heart? Is your body exhausted? Really ask yourself *and really listen*. Listen to what your soul aches for right now and what your body really needs. And please, my sweet friend, whatever you need, give it to yourself. Give yourself the rest. Give yourself the peace and quiet that you have needed for so long. Give yourself time in nature to reconnect with the beautiful world we live in. Give yourself space to simply breathe after everything you have been so busy with. Never go too long without checking in with yourself, my sweet friend. Never get so busy that you do not have any moments left for you.

a beautiful life

This day is part of your story. Whether it is easy or difficult, busy or quiet, extraordinary or ordinary, it plays a part in shaping *you*. So make it a work of art, my sweet friend. Take even just a couple of minutes in the morning to do something that inspires you for the day ahead. Slow down those moments in the morning when the world has not yet woke up and everything is still peaceful and quiet to remind yourself of all the possibilities for the day ahead. As you go about your day, remember that there is magic all around you— even when it feels impossible to find. There are so many reasons to smile and find joy. And as the day comes to an end, take a moment to be grateful for another day. Even if this day was not extraordinary by any means, it played a part in your beautiful life story, and that is something to be wonderfully grateful for.

an extraordinary life

Life is made up of countless little moments all strung together. It's made of the extraordinary moments at the top of the mountains but it's also made of all of the moments spent climbing. It's made of the moments that you thought you were going to break but you held it together a little longer. It's made of the moments you decided to trust and follow your heart despite all of the voices telling you otherwise. It's made of the moments you didn't give up or quit when it would have been so much easier to. And it's made of all of the ordinary moments too. The usual weekday mornings and busy afternoons. The hugs we give our families each day and the meals we share each evening. The nights shared with great friends and deep laughs. The uneventful and quiet workdays— all of those moments make us, *us*. It really is the string of all of our ordinary moments tied together that make this life so extraordinary.

My sweet friend,
it was never meant to be perfect,
it is meant to be real.

a little messy

Life does not always go in a straight line. Things get messy and tangled, and our paths twist and turn in many directions. The right things happen at the wrong time and opportunities get passed by. Some things happen that we just cannot understand in the moment no matter how badly we want an answer. And some things that we wish would happen just never do. Life can be a little messy, but that does not mean that it cannot be wonderful. Because even in the messiness, even in the mistakes and missed chances, even in the midst of not knowing what to do or where to turn, there are still so many beautiful moments. There is still love and joy and light. There is still laughter and kindness. So maybe life is messy. But maybe, it does not need to be anything else. Maybe it is in all of the messiness that we can see all of the things that matter most of all.

8. GETTING LOST

Nikki Banas

Sometimes you must lose yourself
so that you can start all over and
build yourself brand new.

lost

If you come to a place where you are feeling completely and utterly lost, my beautiful friend, listen to me. You will find your way. *You will.* You might be in a place where you feel like there is nowhere to turn, that there is darkness in every direction and not a single flicker of light to be found. But you will find your way. Even if it feels like you can't go back the way you came and you can't keep moving ahead, even when you can't tell right from left and up from down, know that you *will* find your way. You do not need to see the way out right now. You do not need to see the whole plan for the year or the month or the week. You just need to do what you can today. Whatever that looks like. Just do what you can, my beautiful friend. A step in any direction. A decision to not give up. A decision to keep trying no matter what. Because that step— that decision— that is what will change everything. That is how you will find yourself again. *Just one little step.*

finding your way

Your heart always knows the way. It knows the way before you can see the path ahead and before you can see which direction to take. Trust that when your eyes cannot see the way, your heart will guide you in the right direction. Trust that your heart will guide you out of this place and into a place so unimaginably beautiful and breathtaking. Trust that you are about to find the light and your heart is guiding you to it. Your heart does not follow logic or reasoning. It does not guide you with a clear map all perfectly laid out. Your heart guides you deep within. But it requires trust from you that you are headed in the right direction. It requires trust in the things you cannot see yet. Your heart knows that there is so much more out there for you than this place you are in. Your heart knows that there is a greater purpose to all of this and that these dark moments are temporary— no matter how long they feel. Your heart knows that there is so much ahead for you that you cannot even fathom yet, my sweet friend. So whenever you are lost in the dark, instead of squinting into the darkness out there, go within instead. You will find the light to carry you ahead.

understanding

There will be times that you won't be able to understand why things are happening the way that they are. You won't be able to understand why that path ended— why that heartbreak, that person, that job, that opportunity ended. You won't be able to understand why things are taking so long or happening so fast around you. You won't be able to answer why things are unfolding the way they are. But my beautiful friend, maybe you are asking the wrong questions. Maybe you do not need to understand why this is happening. Maybe there just is not an answer out there right now that can help you fully comprehend the depth of the situation that you are in. The truth is that there are many things that you cannot understand until you learn what happens next. You cannot understand why the sun sets until you see it rise and you see the depth and beauty and magnificence of its colors after the long night. You cannot understand why the tides pull away during the day until you see them roar freely through the night. You cannot understand the ending of one story until you begin the sequel... Sometimes, there just won't be an answer to why you are going through this, but my beautiful friend, that's okay. Because in time, you will find the answer. I promise you, *you will*. For now, find it in your heart to let go of needing to understand and trust that it will come in time.

the wrong direction

When you have been traveling down the wrong path for far too long and whether you have just realized it or you have known for a long time, know that you can always change your direction and choose a new path from here. Even if you are knee deep in a wrong choice that you made a while back, even if you feel like you have been drowning for far too long, know that you can still find shore. You can still find peace and comfort and light and all of the things that you deserve in your life. Maybe you have put years into the wrong relationship or into the wrong business. Maybe you gave everything you had for something and it just was not meant to be. My sweet friend, you still hold all of the power in the world to write what will happen next, regardless of what you have already written. You can take a new turn *now*. And maybe you should have done this months or even years ago, but the best option that you have now— the *only* option— is to start changing your course *now*. To turn back or to forge a new way out of here. My sweet friend, you are never stuck on a path that feels like a sinking ship. You are never stuck on a path that leads to a dead-end. You can always go back and try again. You can always create a way out of it. And you can change your path again and again and again, forging new ways whenever you need. So my sweet friend, no matter how far down the wrong path you have gone, begin again now. Start finding your way back home.

Along the Way

My sweet friend,
you really only have two options.
To go or to remain.
To jump or to stay.
To soar or to wonder what it would be like.
My sweet friend,
I hope you always choose to grow.

move on

Sometimes it's the hardest thing in the world to do— to move on. To leave behind something that's not meant for you. To walk away from something you never imagined you would have to walk away from... But sometimes it's the very thing that will set you free. It's the very thing that will allow you to finally start healing and finding your light again. It might take every single ounce of your courage, strength, and willpower to move on and to walk away. It can bring you days or weeks of tears; it can hurt like nothing ever has. It can cut deeper than you thought was possible... But when something is no longer meant for you, my beautiful friend, you *must* let it go. You must not keep carrying the unnecessary weight and the heavy burden. Even if it was wrong or messy or not meant for you, even if it has been a piece of you for longer than you can remember, you cannot continue to hurt yourself for the wrong people and places. You do not have to know what is next yet. You just have to let go in order to make room for all that *is* meant for you. And that really will make all the difference.

Life brings you challenges
to teach you how to overcome.
It brings you impossible waves
to reveal your true strength.
It brings you places that knock you down
to teach you how to rise.

a new perspective

You are never going backwards in life. Life is not a straight line— it is not even close. Life is a winding path that brings you where you need to be— to grow, to become, to be. And if you feel like you keep coming back to the same place, over and over and over again and you just cannot break through, maybe you are not seeking the right thing. Maybe you are missing the whole point of this place that you are in. So life continues to bring you back here until you learn. Until you understand. So look around, my beautiful friend, *really look*. Maybe there is a new direction leading from here, something that you have never done before. Maybe there is someone here that you need to meet. An opportunity to find. And maybe you are simply meant to rest and take a break because you have been going 100 miles an hour for far too long and it is time you hit the brakes. My beautiful friend, if you feel like you are going backwards or you are stuck, know that you aren't. There is just more for you to see here. There is more to learn here, more to understand before you can keep going. So take it all in. Try and allow yourself to see with a different perspective. My beautiful friend, you will find your way. *You always will.*

highs and lows

When you are at a low, remember that that's exactly what it is: a low. It's not permanent, it's not forever. It's a low because things are going to turn around and lead you to so many better things. It's a low because it's a new beginning for beautiful times ahead. Things will start looking up. Light is coming your way, my beautiful friend, remember that. And know that it's okay to be at a low; it's part of this whole thing of being a human— we go through highs and lows, our lives ebb and flow. It's okay to be struggling. It's okay to be down. But it's not okay to think that this low defines you. It's not okay to think that this low is all you are. Because it's not. This low will pass. These tough times will end. Beginnings are coming. Light is coming. Joy is coming. Peace is coming... This is just a low and before you know, you will be soaring again.

Nikki Banas

Acknowledge the rain,
celebrate the rainbows.

rainbows

My beautiful friend, even when you are going through the toughest times, remember that there are still so many beautiful things to be thankful for— things that shine the brightest light in the dark. There are still breathtaking sunrises and incredible sunsets. There are still infinite stars shining in the night sky. There is still a pulse from your heart and air filling your lungs. There is still time to heal and rest and find yourself again. There are still so many people who love and care about you so deeply, and want the best for you. So look for the light and keep looking for the light no matter how hard it gets. Keep loving and cherishing those who light up your dark skies. Keep celebrating the moments when the sun peaks through the clouds. And when you are in the midst of a terrible storm, keep looking for the rainbows— not because you are ignoring the pouring rain and roaring thunder, but because you know that rainbows and rain exist together. Because you know that light is only light because of the dark. Looking for rainbows during the rain was never about ignoring the storm anyways— it is about looking for the light that will carry you through.

darkness

Whenever you go through your darkness, you come out differently. You change. *And that's the point.* That's the point of dark times; they teach you that you *can* rise, that you are stronger than any darkness that may come to you. They teach you that you can go through something like that and still feel so much light on the other side of it. So no matter what you are going through, know that you are going to come out of this. And you are going to come out of this stronger and lighter and freer. You will come out of this a survivor, a *fighter*. You will come out of this a warrior, my sweet friend. You will come out of this a better you— and you will understand yourself so much more. When you are in your darkest moments, know that this is just the beginning. This is where the rebirth happens. This is where the caterpillar transforms into the butterfly. This is where the eagles first test their wings against their shell. This is where seeds are planted. *In the dark.* So yes, you will come out of this darkness differently. And that is exactly the point, my sweet friend. You are going to come out of this with more strength, more confidence in yourself and your ability to rise. You are going to come out of this so much lighter and freer. So stay strong, my sweet friend. *You are so close.*

Along the Way

You will rise, my sweet friend.
I promise you will.

127

Along the Way

You will rise, my sweet friend.
I promise you will.

127

No matter how far away you go,
you will always find your way back home.

phases

No matter how many times you get lost, no matter how many times you get off track or take a wrong turn, you will always return home. Like the moon, you will always find your way back to being full. You will find your way back to feeling whole. Sometimes it takes much longer than you hope or expect. And sometimes it does not happen how you think it will. But you will always return home to where you belong. And maybe you will see that all along you were exactly where you needed to be— that your home was not a place or a person, but that it was within you the entire time.

9. FALLS AND BREAKS

believe in the good

The moments when it feels like nothing good lies ahead are the moments when you need to believe that there is good ahead *the most*. Believe that the light is coming even if all you have seen for days or months or years has been darkness. Believe that good things are coming even when no one else around you does. Believe that better things lie ahead, no matter what. Better relationships, better friendships, better jobs, better health, a better *life*. In those moments when it feels like it is the end, those moments when it feels like nothing good can possibly be ahead, decide to believe it anyway. Decide to see past this chapter and believe in your next chapter. Because these hard moments, these dark days, these are temporary. No matter how permanent they feel, they *will* come to an end. There are still so many beautiful days ahead for you. There are opportunities coming to you that you cannot see yet. There are friendships that will bloom with people that you have not even met yet. Foods that are so deliciously divine that you have not tasted yet. Songs that you will know every word of and belt when you are going seventy down the highway with the windows down and a smile lighting your face. My beautiful friend, there is so much out there for you. No matter your past or what you have faced, no matter your age or the hard times you have faced, there is *still* so much out there that you have not seen yet.

Believe in the good
through every storm,
every trial,
every challenge.

Nikki Banas

falling apart

It is okay for things to not work out. It is okay for plans to change or fail. It is okay for things to get postponed or forgotten. My sweet friend, it really is okay. Things do not work out in order to make space for all of the right things. If something does not work out, it is because there is something else for you— something *better*, something that needs space to come together for you. Sometimes, things do not work out how you had hoped because they were never the right thing for you at all. And by it not working out, it saved you so much heartache and trouble. When things are falling apart, my sweet friend, other things are falling together. You cannot see all of the things getting ready behind the scenes for you. You cannot see all of the right things just waiting for the wrong ones to leave. So let things fall apart, because my sweet friend, other things are falling together.

Trust that when things are falling apart,
others are falling together.

Maybe it won't make sense now or next month or even next year. But maybe we don't need to know...

Maybe we don't always need to understand our past to find love and joy in our todays.

wrong timing

You might meet the perfect person at the wrong time. You might meet the love of your life but the timing just is not right. Maybe you are in different places, maybe you have loose ends that you need to tie up first. Maybe you are simply not ready yet— maybe you still have some growing to do first. But my sweet friend, if the person is right it does not matter if you met them at the wrong time because the right time *will* come. After the distance closes, after you grow and explore yourself first, after you tie up all of your loose ends in a neat little bow, if they are right, they will find their way into your life again, and you into theirs. The hardest part is in the waiting. In all of the days before the right time comes. You have to trust that if they are the right person, you will find your way to each other again. And when the timing becomes right, you will understand why it could not have happened a moment sooner.

trying again and again

You can try again over and over and over again. I mean it, you can try again as many times as humanly possible. Every time you fall, you can stand back up. You can try again every time you slip up, every time you stumble. There is absolutely nothing wrong with trying again or starting over. *Absolutely nothing.* Nobody ever did something perfectly on the first try. Most things take *a lot* of failures before a success. Others might say it is not worth the time and effort, and that you can find something else to do. But my sweet friend, it is worth it because *you* are worth it. Your ideas and dreams and goals are worth trying over and over for because you deserve to bring them to life. No amount of mistakes or failures can keep you from succeeding. Every single person you have ever met has made plenty of mistakes and failed at a lot of things. *That's how we learn and grow.* It is not the mistakes that define you, it is what you do after. How you pick yourself up is what counts... How you try again with what you learned from your mistake and how you double down on your enthusiasm every time. *That* is what counts.

past mistakes

Never, and I mean *never*, continue to beat yourself up for the mistakes you made in the past. Do not be upset about the wrong turns you made when you could not have possibly known better at the time. Do not regret the things you did that made sense at the time. You have to let those go. You have to forgive your past self for all of it. All of the mistakes, all of the mess-ups, all of the losses. You have to be kind and gentle to your past self because they did an awful lot to get you here. And of course they messed up and fell on the way, but those mistakes taught you so much. Those falls strengthened you. Forgive all of your falls and mistakes, my sweet friend. Know that you will make more of them because you are human and that is how we grow and that is okay. Because you can learn and forgive yourself every time.

burn

Sometimes you just need to let it all go. You need to stop gripping onto everything so tightly that your knuckles are white and your soul aches. Sometimes you just need to fall apart. So that you can put yourself back together again. But this time stronger. And softer. Sometimes you need to let yourself feel all of your pain as deep as it cuts so that you can finally let it go and release it. So that you can stop giving it so much power over you. So that you can finally move past it... Sometimes the only way to find your strength is by falling apart first. Like the way the world is peaceful and new after a raging storm. The way the oceans calm after a reckless hurricane. The way the forest is silent in its ash after a wildfire. So let this part of you burn, my beautiful friend. Let go of all of the pain weighing on you. Let go of everything heavy on you. Let it all burn. And then, *then* you can rise.

Feel your pain fully and entirely,
without judgement and then,
my sweet friend,
let it all go.

rise up: pt. 1

When you fall, stand back up. Every. Single. Time. Stand back up. Pick yourself up and get back on your feet. Lift your shoulders up and strong. Get your eyes off the ground and look up at the world above you. *Rise*, my beautiful friend. Rise every time. You can fall ten, twenty, one hundred, *one thousand* times. But my beautiful friend, you can *rise* ten, twenty, one hundred, one thousand times. Never let yourself stay down. Never be the one who gives up on you. Your heart knows you were meant for more than this. Your soul knows that you were never meant to stay down. Trust in your ability to rise every time. Even if it is not fair how you got there, even if you are exhausted from getting back up again and again, even if you think you will just fall again, get back up. You are so much stronger than you could imagine, my beautiful friend. *Nothing* in this world can keep you down.

rise up: pt. 2

It does not matter how often you hit the ground. It does not matter how many times you miss the mark. It does not matter how deep you fall. My beautiful friend, what matters is that you get up and rise, every single time. What matters is that despite how many times you have fallen, despite how much it hurts, you get up and rise anyways. Those are the moments when you find your true strength. Those are the moments that change you deep inside. When you rise, when you rise up every single time, you are showing yourself that you do not stay down. That you will never be defeated. You are showing the universe that you are tougher than the obstacles being thrown at you. That you will never back down. The moment you fall does not matter— not a single bit. Every person falls. Every single one. It is the moment you decide to rise up anyway that changes everything. The moment you decide that you will rise up every single time is the moment you become unstoppable.

Nikki Banas

You are not meant to
carry the weight of the world
on your own two shoulders.
My sweet friend, it's time to set it down.

heaviness

When it is all too heavy, my sweet friend, learn to set it down. Whatever it is. The pressure of trying to fit a week of work into a day. The stress of trying to get things right on the first try. The tiredness from not doing the things that make you feel most alive. The exhaustion from being someone who you're not. The stories that you have been telling yourself and living that you were never meant to have. *Set it all down.* You are not meant to carry the weight of the world on your shoulders. You are not meant to feel this heaviness with every step you take. My sweet friend, you are meant to feel light. You are meant to be free and joyful and *alive*. You are meant for reckless laughter. You are meant to feel joy in every new day. You are meant for so much more than this heaviness my sweet friend. I think it is time you finally set it down.

pick yourself back up

Learn how to pick yourself up, my beautiful friend. Learn how to pick yourself up after even the hardest fall. Learn how to carry yourself forward during the moments when all you want to do is collapse onto the ground. Learn how to pick yourself up again and again and again. Because my brave friend, you are worth fighting for. There will be a lot of moments that knock you down, causing you to lose all of your balance. There will be times when nobody else will be there to help pick you up. There will be times where the only thing that is keeping you going is *you*. And in those moments, you have to decide. You have to decide whether you will give up, or if you will stand up. You have to decide that you are worth standing up for. You have to decide that you will not give up on you, not now, and *not ever*. The moments that you decide to keep trying are the moments that change the course of your life, my brave friend. Those are the moments that build you stronger. Those are the moments that add fuel to your fire. Those are the moments that show your true heart and your true character.

You are worth fighting for.
You are worth the struggle.
You are worth standing back up for,
again and again and again.

whole

You are whole, my sweet friend. Just as you are. The pieces of you that you think are broken are really the pieces that make you whole. The pieces that you think are missing are not missing at all. There is nothing missing about you, my sweet friend. The things that you think are flaws are the things that make you so beautifully you. The cracks and spaces of imperfection is where the real beauty lies. None of us are perfect. We are all a little broken and messy. We all have stories that we would rather not tell. We all have heartbreaks and pains that never really fully healed. But that is what makes us so beautifully human. That we experience all of it— the deep joys of life and the heartbreaking sadness. The indescribable moments of happiness and vivid color when our world lights up. The devastating moments of pain when our world falls apart. That is what makes us, *us*. That is what makes us strong. And beautiful. And powerful. And *gentle*. That is what makes us whole. Not that we are perfect or flawless or have everything in order, but that despite everything that does not work, we are still here making our lives beautiful anyway.

sit with yourself

When your heart feels heavy and the world is resting heavy atop your shoulders, when your stomach twists and turns and aches, my beautiful friend sit with yourself. Sit with the feelings stirring deep inside of you. Sit with the hard emotions and the thoughts that come with them... You do not need to understand them, you do not need to make sense of why you're feeling this way. You do not need to work them out like there is an easy answer at the end... My beautiful friend, you only need to sit with them. You only need to allow yourself room to feel them entirely. You only need to give yourself space and make room in your heart. You do not need to solve any feeling or figure anything out. You only need to sit with yourself.

Oh if only you could see
just how beautiful you truly are.
The way your eyes light up when you smile,
the way your face beams when
you talk about what you love,
the way your excitement is contagious.
Oh if only could see you,
my beautiful friend.

wonderfully yours

You are so wonderfully you. Do not look at them, my sweet friend, you are not them. Your path is yours. There is no reason it should look exactly like theirs. Not a single one. You have your own path to walk, your own course to chart. And you are meant to do it in your own way. If you were meant to be anywhere else, you would be. Do not worry about looking around at them. Look at the beautiful path you have already walked and how you have grown. Look at who you have become and all that you have learned about yourself. When you spend time thinking about the *should have been's*, you lose time to look at all that is. You lose time to see all of the beautiful things right in front of you. So maybe you are not where you want to be yet. Maybe you are not who you want to be yet or you do not have the things you want yet. But you are in the place you need to be now to get there. And that, my sweet friend, is enough.

Nikki Banas

inner peace

You will find the inner peace you have been looking for. You will find the healing you have been seeking and freedom from the pain you have been dealing with... Sometimes you just have to let go of everything else for a little while in order to return to you, to ground yourself again, to find your center again... Sometimes you just have to give yourself the time, the space, and the break you need from everything. From the people who have been wearing on you. The work that has been draining you. The environment that has been hurting you. Sometimes you have to pause and turn down all of the sounds out there to listen to everything that is going on within you. To listen to what your heart has been begging for— whether it is more time to rest, more nature, more love, more gentleness. Whatever it is, my sweet friend, give that to yourself. Give yourself the kindness you need and deserve. Give yourself the love you have been aching for and know that it needs to come from you first. Give yourself what you need, my sweet friend, and return to your true self.

always gentle

My beautiful friend, be gentle with yourself and your soul. Be kind to yourself when you feel like you have failed or when you feel like you just cannot get things right. Know that your mistakes only feel big right now, but soon they will just be little moments of the past. And know that they do not define your future; you can still grow and become and be whoever you want to be. Be gentle with yourself... Be one of the people who believes in you wholeheartedly. There is plenty of discouragement out there, so create a space of encouragement within your own heart. Become the voice that always says you can, the voice that has faith in you regardless of what others say. Be gentle with yourself, my beautiful friend. Be gentle especially when you are hurting and when you are down. *Always gentle*... You really are doing great.

No matter what,

we go on.

we go on

When you are tucked into your covers after a long day, my beautiful friend, remember this: *we always go on...* You have gone through so much already. You could fill countless shelves of books with all of your stories. You could talk endlessly about the people and places, the struggles and victories that have helped shape who you are. And after everything you have seen and everything you have been through, you always went on. It might not have been pretty, it might not have been perfect, but you always went on anyway. You made it through a lot. You made mistakes and you gave less than your best sometimes. You might not have always been your kindest or best self, but... You still went on. And over and over, no matter what comes your way next, you will continue to go on. Today, tomorrow, next week, next month, you will keep doing everything that you can, and you will go on.

10. THE PEAK

Nikki Banas

take it all in

My beautiful friend, this is the part where you celebrate yourself. You have just reached the peak— you finished the big project, you crossed the finish line. You did the thing that you thought you couldn't do and you overcame so much on the way. My beautiful friend, you climbed your mountain. *You reached the peak.* You climbed all the way up. It was not easy— my gosh— it was not easy. You hit roadblocks and bumps and had some falls. You had to switch directions and make a few turnarounds. You had to grow in ways that you never thought were even possible, but my beautiful friend look at you now! Look at where you are. Look at the mountain you just climbed. Look out in every direction around you. Be so proud of yourself for getting here. Be so proud of the person that you became on the way up. Be so proud of how far you have come. Slow it all down, forget about what comes next, and just take it all in, my beautiful friend. Take in the magnificent views all around you. Savor the feeling of knowing you just did something incredible. Allow the joy and pride to overflow from your heart out into the world. You did it. My beautiful friend, *you did it.*

158

Along the Way

I am so very proud of you,
my brave friend,
for how far you have come,
for how much you have grown.

Live a life worth celebrating.

celebrate yourself

Celebrate yourself, my sweet friend. Celebrate who you have become and everything that you have done. Celebrate all of your hard work. Celebrate all of the long nights and the early mornings that you poured yourself into your work. Celebrate every moment that you wanted to give up but you stood back up and continued on anyway. Celebrate *you*, my beautiful friend. Go out to your favorite restaurant. Bring your favorite people and laugh the night away. Go to your favorite store and treat yourself to that thing you have been eyeing for *so* long. Go swim in the ocean, camp in the mountains, kayak in the lake, explore the city. Wherever you have been dreaming of, go there. Dance through the streets and sing your heart out. Celebrate yourself, my sweet friend. Celebrate everything you have done and the incredible person that you have become.

this life

Never go too long without celebrating this life. Never get so caught up in the day-to-day busyness, the worries and troubles, the comparison and doubts that you forget just how wonderful it is to be here. Never get so caught up that you forget to notice all of the blessings worth celebrating right around you. Celebrate those who care about you so deeply, the ones who always lift you up and help you. Celebrate all of the little victories in your day-to-day to-do lists and the things you love to do each day. Celebrate all of the things that make the little moments of life so wonderful and vibrant too— your favorite shows and books, clothes and foods. Celebrate all of the growth you have done and continue to do—all of the ways you are becoming and reaching and stretching. My sweet friend, this life holds so much worth celebrating.

look at you now

Pause and breathe, my brave friend. Let air fill every inch of your lungs and let it all back out into the world. You have come so far. Look who you have become. You have grown so much and walked so far. You have crossed vast oceans and traveled through the dark. You have climbed many mountains and you have had more than your fair share of tumbles on the way. You have come a long way, my brave friend. *Look at you now,* with this chapter behind you, hills and valleys and all. Allow yourself to pause and breathe it all in before you move onto your next chapter. Breathe in who you have become and all the ways you have grown. Breathe out all of your faults and mistakes. Breathe in the strength you have gained through it all and breathe out any regrets. You have done so much, my brave friend, just look at you now.

11. ALONG THE WAY

Nikki Banas

No one will ever
be able to take away
who you became
through it all.

tallest mountains

As you conquer both the mountains out there and the ones within you, my beautiful friend, I hope you find that even the tallest ones cannot scare you or intimidate you to walk away— to not even try. I hope that no dream is too grand, no obstacle is too big, and no distance is too far for you to say yes to. And someday, I hope that not only do they not scare you, but that the tallest peaks and greatest journeys *excite* you for the adventure and possibility that they hold within their winding paths. I hope that the peak hidden behind the clouds tickles your soul to want to take on the challenge and experience its grand adventure. I hope you always see the biggest challenges as a collection of little and manageable goals — each of which you are completely and entirely capable of doing. I hope you see that all it takes is just one little step— over and over again— and that when you continue putting one foot ahead of the other, no distance is too far. Most of all, my beautiful friend, I hope you climb the tallest mountains you can find because you deserve to discover and experience how wildly capable you truly are. You deserve to believe in yourself and your potential because my beautiful friend, it is truly *limitless*.

beautiful moments

Throughout it all, I hope you come to find that your path is more beautiful than you could have ever imagined. I hope you see that there is so much life to be found in every moment. I hope you see that there is so much to be found in every twist and turn, and around every corner. I hope you look for the beauty in the sky even during the thunderous storms. I hope you look for it in the flowers before they bloom because even their delicate buds hold so much grace and wonder. And I hope that when it is hard to find the light and magic that you go out of your way to seek it. To put your foot down and say, I am going to find the magic in every day because this life truly is a gift. And when you look and look and look and there is only darkness and gloom all around you, my beautiful friend, I hope you *create* beautiful moments of light and magic. I hope you create the joy you want to feel and bring the smile that you want to share. I hope that you find that beautiful moments exist everywhere and that you will always be able to find them. *Always.*

No matter where
you decide to go or
what you choose to do,
live deeply,
my beautiful friend.

always forward

When your path feels dark and rigid and harsh, and you keep losing your footing and fall down, I hope you stand back up every time. And not only stand back up, but stand up taller with each fall. I hope that every cut and scrape reminds you that no fall can keep you from moving ahead. And that no stumble makes the journey worth stopping all together. I hope your scars remind you not of the times that you fell, but of all the times that you rose— all of the times you stood back up anyway. My brave friend, I hope you always know that you are stronger than you could ever imagine. You are stronger than any fall, any break, and any obstacle that comes to you. Because when you are in a hard place, you really only have two options: stay down or stand back up and keep marching forward. Stay down or rise. Remain or *go forward*. And I hope that you always remember to keep moving forward because no matter how dark, no matter how rigid the path, no matter how many falls it takes to get there, you can always find a clearing full of shining light if you just continue marching on.

No matter how hard or how badly you fall,
decide to stand up tall every single time.

The strength within you will always be greater than
anyone or anything that tries to break you.

strong heart

My courageous friend, I hope you always remember that you are made of incredible strength and grit. Whenever life puts you under immense pressure, your strength within can withstand it. Your strength can surpass that of *anything* out there. Every obstacle, every challenge, every setback... And whenever you feel like giving up, whenever you feeling like throwing in the towel because you just cannot keep going for another second, my courageous friend, let your brave and strong heart carry you through. Because your courageous heart will be what pushes you forward when everything seems to pull you backward. With every tough moment and hard climb, I hope you find it easier and easier to trust yourself, your strength, and your potential even when the world does not. I hope that you believe in your strength not only in the moments when it is easy to feel it, but in all of the moments that it feels nearly impossible to.

Nikki Banas

belonging

I hope you always know that you belong. No matter how different or out of place you feel, I hope you know that there *is* space just for you. And more than anything, my sweet friend, I hope that you *take up that space*. I hope that you let your true colors shine instead of hiding them within. And that you always know it is better to stand out than to paint yourself a different color than who you truly are. Because my sweet friend, we *need* your colors. The world needs your unique gifts... The world needs you just as you are, not a muted or toned down version, but the real and authentic you. And even when you are not understood or heard, even when you make mistakes or mess up, I hope that you continue to let your true self free. Because I promise you, my sweet friend, *you* belong here.

a love for life

Most of all, I hope you find everything you are looking for not just at the top of your mountain, but all along the way too. And I hope you find everything you never knew you were looking for, too. I hope your path is full of breathtaking moments and beautiful surprises. I hope that your path is filled with moments that light you up from the inside out— moments full of so much joy that you just cannot contain it and it spills out into the world around you. My beautiful friend, I hope that throughout it all, you find a boundless love for *life* itself. Love for yourself even before you have 'made it'. Love for the people around you even if they are imperfect and make mistakes too. Love for your days and how you get to spend them. I hope you find a boundless love for life— for the extraordinary moments and the ordinary ones. For the boring days and the hectic ones. Because it's all part of your beautiful story... *All of it.*

Nikki Banas

May you find everything you are looking for
not just at the top of your mountains,
but all along the way too.

With love,

Nikki Banas

ACKNOWLEDGEMENTS

I am deeply thankful for all those who made this book possible. Thank from the bottom of my heart. I am only me because of *you*.

To you, beautiful reader—Thank you for picking up this book and for reading it all the way here to these final pages. Thank you from the bottom of my heart for following along with my own journey and reading my words. I hope you found so much love and light tucked inside of these pages.

To Dennis—Thank you so much for your endless support. Thank you for believing in me and every single dream of mine. I simply would not be me, without *you*.

To my family— Thank you for the life you've given me and for all of your love, encouragement, and laughter.

To my beautiful friends—I am so blessed to have you in my life. Thank you for inspiring me every day to become a better me.

MEET THE AUTHOR

Author of *Shine from Within*, Nikki Banas found her love for writing at a young age. After receiving a journal as a gift as a young girl, she found so much joy and freedom within its blank pages. After sharing her first few letters of encouragement under the name *Walk the Earth* on Instagram and Pinterest, her words quickly spread, touching the hearts of hundreds of thousands with her raw, honest, and encouraging words.

Nikki resides outside of Chicago and spends her time writing, exploring nature, and being with her family.

You can purchase her books and other treasures with her writing at: NikkiBanas.com. You can connect with her on Instagram and Pinterest @WalkTheEarthWriter

Made in United States
North Haven, CT
03 September 2023

41077369R00114